Mission and Vision Statement Renewal Workbook for Churches

Rev. Jessica Crane Munoz

Acknowledgments

I wish to thank my family, friends, and the Presbyterian Church of Vinton, IA for their support and assistance. And my colleagues, especially those on the Presbytery of East Iowa Vision and Renewal Task Force, who encouraged this endeavor.

Table of Contents

Acknowledgments 2

Introduction 4

Session 17

Session 2 15

Session 3 23

Session 4 29

    Mission statement 33

Session 5 41

Session 6 49

Conclusion 51

About the Author 52

Introduction

This workbook is intended to be used by churches that are looking critically at their existing Mission and/or Vision statements. It can also be used by churches in revising their statements or building new statements.

In six sessions, it will lead you step-by-step through the creating, or re-creating, of your mission statement. It does not provide "best practices" for developing your mission statement. Rather, it is a short and practical guide to help you review or create a statement by examining your priorities as individuals and as a whole congregation.

The workbook is intended to be used by a Session (or board, for non-PCUSA users) in five sessions, with a meeting of the congregation near the end of the project before the finalization of statements. Each session can be held in conjunction with a regular board meeting or at a separate time. At least 45-60 minutes is suggested for each workbook session.

There is no leader's guide, though it may require some prep work on the part of the Moderator and/or Clerk to provide materials (white boards, markers, previous mission statements to hand out) at each session.

Session/board participants should be given folders/binders at the first session to help them organize information for subsequent meetings. The materials build upon each other.

So why re-envision your Mission statement?

Churches often only look at their existing mission and vision statements in times of crisis and transition. By looking at statements during times of stability, congregations can set a path to walk along, and set goals to grow as an organization and as a body of Christ.

This process is an act of discipleship: how do we become the best Christian body that we can be, in this time and in this place? We lead, through prayer, discernment, and by marking out a path for the church that is faithful, clear, and relevant to the current life and climate of the church.

God's blessing to you as you enter this endeavor.

Pastor Jessica

Session 1

We begin by doing some individual, paired, and group exercises to consider and verbalize core values. Core values can be defined as those things (principles, ideas, things, morals, guiding beliefs) which are central the church. Consider core values to be the guiding principles that determine the behavior and actions of the congregation.

Core values can range from intangible beliefs to concrete items or groups. It would not be unusual to see a grouping of core values that included both *youth* (tangible, concrete) and *knowledge* (intangible). Both are appropriate as they both can simultaneously central to the makeup of the church.

Exercises for Determining Core Values: to be filled out <u>in pairs</u>, with partners asking each other these questions and recording the answers for the other. *Swap workbooks* with your partner so that the answers you record for them will be written in their workbook.

1. How do you describe your church? 5 words

2. How do others in your town describe your church? 5 words

3. What church leaders, modern, historical or biblical, do you admire and why? Name 3

4. What are the 3 best compliments you have ever heard made about the church?

5. What is the one thing your church does best?

6. What is one thing your church doesn't do well?

7. If there is one thing you wish you never had to do again at church, what would it be?

8. If there was one thing you want your (children, grandchildren, spouse, friend) to learn at church, what would it be?

When everyone has finished, return your partner's notebook, and then reconvene as a large group. Discuss as a <u>large group</u> the results of your question/answer time.

Record common themes or important concepts from each question on a large whiteboard, newsprint, or media that is large enough for everyone to see. Answers to these questions will be needed for Session 4.

A Voting Exercise: <u>As individuals</u>

Write down ten words that identify what you perceive your church's values to be:

1.	
2.	
3.	
4.	
5.	
6.	
7.	
8.	
9.	
10.	

Now, take your priority list and rank them in this way:

Take Word One and compare it to Word Two. If one ranks higher, give it a tally mark. If it does not rank higher, leave the space in front of Word One blank but give a tally to Word Two.

Then compare Word One to Word Three. If One ranks higher, give it another tally mark. Move down the page in this way, comparing Word One to each word on your list. After comparing Word One, you should have 9 total tallies in the boxes.

Here is an example:

1.	Teaching
2.	Mission
3.	Fellowship
4.	Outreach
5.	Worship
6.	Sacraments

Teaching vs. Mission	Teaching less important	Tally in Mission box
Teaching vs. fellowship	Teaching more important	Tally in Teaching box
Teaching vs. outreach	Teaching less important	Tally in Outreach box
Teaching vs. worship	Teaching less important	Tally in Worship box

| Teaching vs. Sacraments | Teaching less important | Tally in Sacraments box |

1.	Teaching	|
2.	Mission	|
3.	Fellowship	
4.	Outreach	|
5.	Worship	|
6.	Sacraments	|

Do the same with the next word, Word Two, and moving down through each word.

Mission vs. Fellowship	Mission more important	Tally in Mission box
Mission vs. Outreach	Mission less important	Tally in Outreach box
Mission vs. Worship	Mission less important	Tally in Worship box
Mission vs. Sacraments	Mission more important	Tally in Mission box

1.	Teaching	|
2.	Mission	|| |
3.	Fellowship	
4.	Outreach	||
5.	Worship	||
6.	Sacraments	

When finished, count up the tally marks for each word. Then rank them from highest to lowest.

Core Value Chart and Ranking

	Word or Phrase:	Tally:
1.		
2.		
3.		
4.		
5.		
6.		
7.		
8.		
9.		
10.		

What word ranks the highest on your value list? What is second? Write your list below in order that you have prioritized them. It is not uncommon for two Words to have the same value. You may find that while you originally thought a word would have high value, it pales in comparison to other words you chose.

Likewise, you may have two very similar words that rank differently based on your personal conceptions of how it is understood in the church.

Voting Exercise: As a Group

Compare your top words and lists <u>as a group,</u> coming up with some core similarities in words. On a flip-chart or large white board, record your group's list of words and phrases that are of the highest priority.

This important list of words will help keep you focused will be used in subsequent sessions to help prioritize portions of your Mission and Vision statements. In section 4, you will use your list as you being to build your Mission and Vision statement.

Session 2

Differentiating between Mission Statement and Vision Statement

What a Vision statement is:
- Brief: one sentence or less. Sometimes only a phrase
- Big-picture: a hope or a dream of what the organization is about or what it can be
- Something that everyone can agree on
- Can be the same as a slogan: a way to advertise who you are – promoting yourself on a t-shirt, bumper sticker, etc.

What it looks like:
- "Showing Love, Service, and Compassion in a Changing World"
- "A Family of Believers Dedicated to Serving Christ"
- "Come Grow With Us"

What a Mission statement is:
- Concise plans, goals, actions for a group
- Also big-picture but with more details about areas of church programming; leaves out the minutae but addresses in broad strokes the whole of the organization

- Can be broken down into specific segments within a larger community
- Verb-oriented: "To create" "To change" "To renew" "Teaching" "Growing"

How to begin building a Mission Statement:

<u>As a group,</u> brainstorm verbs and nouns associated with your ministry. Write them in separate columns on a white board, or separate sheets of presentation paper.

For a great list of nouns, visit your top listed core values from the first session. However, nouns do not need to appear on your core value list in order to be listed below. This list of nouns associated with ministry can be persons, things, ideas, places that are everyday components of ministry or ideals about where you want ministry to grow.

Some words, like "Sanctuary" for example, can have both spatial (actual locational) meaning as well as ideological meaning (as in a place where people feel safe). It may be necessary to clarify this later during group discussion. Or it can be that both meanings are appropriate in the context of your ministry.

Verbs of Ministry	Nouns of Ministry

Conversation: "What do we want people to know about who we are?"

Each person should create favorite pairings of your verbs and nouns. Individuals should retain their list of verbs and nouns for use in Session 4.

As a Group, choose your top 3 favorite verb/noun pairs. Examples: "Ministering people" and "Growing here".

As a group to determine 3-5 core areas of ministry within your church. For some churches, this will already be known and established. Other churches may have to determine their primary areas of ministry.

Often, a church budget is a way to visualize how your ministry is categorized. Funding is often a key indicator to how ministry is prioritized within a church.

For example, you may identify several components that can be listed under a larger heading of Christian education (adult studies, Sunday school, vacation bible school, etc.). Each could be an area of ministry on its own, but the goal is to examine how your overall programming is organized.

1.	
2.	
3.	
4.	
5.	

Talk about specific short-term and long-term goals in each area of ministry. List them.

Then rank them in order of priority for ministry. Which goals help you to live into your core values? Which goals help you achieve where you want ministry to be focused in the future of the organization?

Area of Ministry:	Top Priority for being the church in this area of ministry
Example: Sunday School	Equipping teachers with great curriculum and supplies

How to begin building a Vision statement

As a group, look at your top three Core Values. What are they? (These answers about Core Values will be used in section 4.)

Then, in a group brainstorming session (limit to 3-4 mins per question) ask these following questions of the group:

- Who do you want people to say you are as an organization?

Look back to your first session:
- How did you think people described your organization?
- How would you like that to change or stay the same?

Things to consider when building your statement:
- Does it give people hope?
- Does it inspire people to action?
- Would you want to be part of a group who affirmed this statement?
- Does it actually say something about who you are, or does it just "sound nice". If it doesn't say something about who you are, go back to your core values conversation.

The best, and worst, part of building a Vision statement is that it takes a lot of brainstorming and conversation to come up with something meaningful.

Make sure:
- Everyone agrees with the statement. While your mission statement might have components that not everyone loves, your vision statement should be affirmed by everyone invested in building it.

- It is short and concise, but it says a great deal about your organization.

For a corporate look at Vision statements and Mission statements, see online:

http://ctb.ku.edu/en/table-of-contents/structure/strategic-planning/vision-mission-statements/main

Session 3

Preparing: moderator or clerk should bring copies of existing and former mission statements to pass out to each individual.

What is your current existing mission statement?

What is your current existing vision statement?

Do you have prior mission and/or vision statements that you can refer to?

As a group, pass out copies of current and prior statements for the group. Read statements aloud.

In pairs: What key word/words stand out in your current statement?

Do they stand out because:

- They reflect current values
- They do not reflect current values
- They seem irrelevant to ministry here
- Our context has/has not changed

Do any of the key word/s overlap with the Core Value words you established in session one.

In pairs, compare and contrast the areas of ministry lined out in your existing and previous mission statements to the verbs and nouns section from session two.

List overlapping verbs & nouns:

Verbs:	Nouns:

Now list verbs and nouns that you LIKE from your current and prior statements that did not appear in your conversation from last time:

Thinking in terms of the 3-5 ministry categories that you established in session two:

- Does your existing mission statement address the areas of ministry that you identified last time? What areas are the same? Different?

- If your existing and/or previous mission statement(s) does not specifically define mission areas, can you at least identify various areas of ministry as you read the statement?

- How does your existing mission statement address these areas of ministry?

    o In the same way that your conversation last week did?
    o In a different way?
    o How has your ministry perhaps grown or changed since the mission statement was written?

- Select, as best you can determine, the ways in which your existing statement addresses each area of ministry that you have identified.

-

As a group:

On a white board, as a group pick words/phrases you like from your existing mission statement and list them. Then pick words/phrases that you do not like or that seem irrelevant.

While it is not necessary to list them separately, it is helpful for the group to identify areas of program, ministry, etc. that no longer are relevant to the current organization.

Identifying words that are irrelevant can seem like a negative practice. But this is not true: organizations are meant to grow, change, and develop over time. There may be many reasons behind why something that was relevant 10, 15, or 20 years ago was appropriate then but may not be now.

Discuss and identify areas of ministry from your existing statement.

Discuss ways in which your church and ministry have changed since the statement was written. Discuss ways in which your church and ministry are the same as when then statement was written.

List your favorite parts of your current statement, based on the areas of ministry. Save this list for use in section four.

Session 4

Today we lay out the pieces that you have put together in sessions 1-3.

Gather the materials that you have compiled to date, and have them easily accessible as you work together to build your mission and vision statements.

For some, this will be a completely new statement, while for others it is a reworking of existing statements.

From Section One you'll need:
- Group results of conversation 'how you describe your church'
- Group results of conversation 'how others in your town describe your church'
- Group results of conversation 'one thing you want your (children, grandchildren, spouse friend) to learn at church
- List of Core Values key words and phrases that rank highest for individuals and group

From Section Two you'll need:
- Group top three favorite verb/noun pairs. Have individual verbs and nouns also available in case further brainstorming is needed in this area.

- List of your 3-5 core areas of ministry within your church
- Short-term and long-term goals in each area of ministry,
- Conversation notes from group conversation: 'what do we want people to know about who we are?' in session two.

From Section Three you'll need:
- Existing mission and vision statements
- Any former mission and/or vision statements
- List of overlapping verbs and nouns from your current/former statements and the verbs and nouns you came up with in Two
- Lists of verbs and nouns the group liked but that do not appear in the current statement
- Identified areas of ministry from current statement
- Your group list of favorite parts of your current statement, based on identified areas of ministry

Split your large group into two equally-divided smaller groups of individuals.

Now, you will pour over the data you compiled, and will examine what the highest priorities are for your church in ministry.

Reminder: Mission statements are big picture, but they also have a goal-setting tone to them. Vision statements are also big picture, but are short, concise, and give someone just a few words about the organization.

Questions for conversation in your two groups:

What have you identified as your current areas of ministry?

What is the highest priority in each area?

Look at your verb and noun pairs. Which verb and which noun would best summarize your priority in this area?

For example, if Teaching is an area and training Sunday school teachers is your highest priority, your verb and noun pair may be "equipping leaders".

Chart: Area of Ministry Priorities

	Area of Ministry	Highest Priority	Verb and Noun pair
1			
2			
3			
4			
5			

Remember that in mission statements, not all members will agree equally on priorities. It is your goal to summarize as best you can the direction and inclination of the body of the church. This is about setting a general tone, and a vision for what the church can and may be/become.

Next, take your list of your favorite parts of your existing mission statement.

Are they reflected at all in your chart above?

What is missing?

If something stands out, list it here so you keep it for later.

Take a look at your core values.

How are your core values reflected, or not reflected, in the ministry and priorities chart? If there is not a strong overlap between core values and your verb-noun pair, re-examine ways in which your core values can be exemplified within your ministry areas and priorities. Use a clean chart if necessary.

Now you have the areas of your ministry, your goals in each area, your verb and noun pairs, and your core values identified within each area.

<u>As a large group</u>, come back together with two completed charts from your smaller groups.

Because you brainstormed about your areas of ministry together, these areas should be identical or nearly identical. Using the two charts, you can build your mission statement components:

Mission statement – what it will look like

Your introduction will go here. You will do this work later when you work on your vision statement.

We strive to:

Look at #1 under Area of Ministry Priority Chart: what is your first identified area of ministry?

Take verb/noun pair from area of ministry #1 and create a sentence based on the first identified area of ministry from group one. List this sentence now on the Areas of Ministry Chart found later in this session.

Now, select another verb and noun pair from session two or from your small group conversation earlier in this session and use this verb/noun pair to create a second sentence based on the top identified goal.

Look at #2 under Area of Ministry. What is your second identified area of ministry?

Again, build a sentence based on each group's verb/noun pair and top identified goal. Then, select a second verb/noun pairing from either your small group conversation earlier in this session or from your verb and noun list compiled in session two.

Repeat for areas of ministry #3-5.

Example: We strive to teach the gospel to children and adults by *equipping leaders* and training teachers. We *provide resources* and invite parents to walk alongside us in our teaching.

Once you have completed your Areas of Ministry exercise, review your list from session three which identified important parts of your current or former mission statements.

Do these important ideas show up here? If not, should they be included? Or could they be used as an introduction to your statement, or as a closing statement to your statement?

Discuss as a group.

Chart: Areas of Ministry

Area of Ministry:	Sentences 1 & 2
1.	1.
	2.
2.	1.
	2.
3.	1.
	2.
4.	1.
	2.
5.	1.
	2.

Introduction to your Mission Statement:

Look at your core values. What is your number one value? What is number two? List them here:
1.
2.

Look back at Session One: What did you identify as the most important things that you want people to know about your church? And what is the one thing that you hope people gain from church? List them here.

Sentence building:

Tell people what your #1 core value is in a way that identifies it as the most important piece of your ministry.

Example – core value of Wisdom;
"We are a body of believers who seek wisdom."

Tell people what your #2 core value is in a way that identifies it as having high importance.

Example – core value of Outreach;
"We desire to do outreach in our community, and in the world."

Next, tell people the most important thing you want people to know about your church:

"We are an open, welcoming, and diverse group of people."

And finally, tell people what you hope they'll gain from your church:

"We want to show Christ's love to each person who enters our doors.

Putting it together:

- + Core value one sentence
- + Core value two sentence
- + What you want them to know sentence
- + What you hope they'll gain sentence
- + Ministry area 1 two sentences
- + Ministry area 2 two sentences
- + Ministry area 3 two sentences
- + Ministry area 4 two sentences (if 4th area was identified)
- + Ministry area 5 two sentences (if 5th area was identified)
- + Any important piece kept from previous statement that did not fit an area of ministry.

Here's the example we have built:

We are a body of believers who seek wisdom. We desire to do outreach in our community, and in the world. We are an open, welcoming, and diverse group of people [and] we want to show Christ's love to each person who enters our doors.

We strive to teach the gospel to children and adults through equipping leaders and training teachers. We provide resources and invite parents to walk alongside us in our teaching.

A Vision Statement Emerges:

Looking at your top two core values sentences, does anything stand out that might serve as a vision statement?

- Believers seeking wisdom
- Reaching out in the community and the world
- A body of believers, [learning] and doing outreach [learning substituted for seek wisdom]
- A body of believers in the world

Brainstorm here your possibilities using your top two core values. If nothing rises to the top, go back and examine core value #3 for potential.

List potentials:

What suits your organization best? Things to consider:

- Does it say something about who you are?
- Does it inspire hope?
- Would you want this as a personal slogan?
- Could you wear it on a t-shirt?

Remember – this is big-picture and generalized. Don't get too specific here. Take a vote to determine which phrase is best-liked by the whole group. And there you have it!

Session 5

This is an important congregational participation component to building your mission and visioning statements. It should be occur after Sessions One-Four, but before mission and visioning statements are finalized. It leads the congregation through many of the questions that have already been examined by the session/board and then it presents the work that has been done.

You will need a way to present two sets of data.

This gathering need not be long but with enough time allowed to bring the congregation into the conversation, build enthusiasm around the new statements, and hear their ideas. By including the congregation in the process, the church builds community ownership of the statements.

Select someone to lead the discussion who can encourage participation, and yet firmly move from one point of conversation to another. It is best if the person leading the discussion has been a participant in all four previous sessions.

While the minister may be present and encouraging through this process, you may choose to have someone other than the minister leading the congregational discussion. This sends a message to the congregation that it is the leadership body as a whole, and not just the minister, that is working toward the formation of the mission and vision statements.

Read the questions in each section below aloud to the congregation. Record responses separately for side-by-side comparison.

I. Identity

1. What do you want people to know about the church?

2. What do people in the community say about the church? (allow for any answers)

    a. Are these things positive or negative?

    b. Now focus on the positive (Leader: re-direct energy toward only positive/uplifting, or neutral, answers)

3. What do you want people to learn or experience while they're here?

4. What is the most important thing for you about the church?

II. Values

Next, let's brainstorm about what you see as the words which describe best the words or phrases that identify the values of the church. For example, one value may be "teaching" or another value may be "mission outreach".

1. Build a list of at least 20 words and phrases that describe the values held by the church. (Recorder: take note/star any words that are often-repeated.)

2. Narrow your list. Are there any words or phrases that are similar enough that they can be combined or one selected over the other? For example, wisdom and knowledge are very similar. While they are not the same, can you pick one that better summarizes the congregation? Eliminate and pare word list down until you have 8-12 identified words that best describe values held by the church.

3. Take your narrowed list of words and reflect on your Identity questions from I. regarding what you want people to know, learn, or experience while they are at church. Make stars by words that are reflected in what you want people to know/learn/experience.

a. Next, take your list of things that are most important for you in church. Make stars by words that overlap.

5. When you have an identified list of 8-12 words that the congregation has compiled, display the list of words the congregation came up with and put it side by side with the list that was created by your board/session in Session One. Are the lists similar?

   a. What is the same?

   b. What is different?

III. Areas of Ministry

1. Brainstorm out loud with your congregation about what areas of ministry they identify in the church. Start by giving generalized examples of areas of ministry – not so specific that it jeopardizes conversation, but enough that they understand how to identify an area of ministry. Use these examples or others relevant to your context: *Youth Ministry, Worship, Mission, Outreach.* Ask

2. Once you have a list of 10-15 areas of ministry, combine those areas that clearly overlap. For example, if one area of ministry is teaching, and another is Sunday school,

and another is youth programming, they may be summarized as "Christian Education".

3. Work to narrow your list to approximately 5 designated areas of ministry.

4. Then ask the congregation to identify 2-3 goals in each section, prioritizing them with #1 being the most important goal.

You should have a chart with 5 identified Areas of Ministry and 2-3 goals per area.

Show the Areas of Ministry that your board/session created in Sessions 1-4 and set it beside the congregation's identified Areas of Ministry. Then reveal the goals in each of the areas for comparison.

1. Discuss how the areas of ministry are the same, and how they are different.

2. Discuss which goals are the same, and which are different. Are these just linguistic differences, or a difference in priority?

IV. Existing and Former Mission and Vision Statements

If you do not have an existing or former mission statement, move to section V.

1. Present your existing (and former) mission statement and vision statements. Before you read the statements aloud, ask the congregation to listen closely for the relevance of the statement(s), and what they do and do not like about the statement(s).

2. Talk about the current relevance, things the congregation likes about it, and things the congregation does not like using the questions below.

   Note: by presenting your existing mission statement after the values and ministry areas conversation, you eliminate a biasing influence that the existing statement may have on your new outlook.

Questions to ask the congregation about the existing statement

1. What is your favorite part of the current statement?

2. Does it identify areas of ministry?

3. Are any pieces of it irrelevant or no longer right for the current context?

4. What is your least favorite part of the statement?

Repeat this for each statement you have.

V. Work to Date from Sessions 1-4

Present the drafts of the statements created by the session/board in Session 4. Read it aloud.

1. Do the proposed statements reflect the church's identity?

2. Are the values of the church reflected?

3. Are important areas of ministry identified?

4. Does the proposed statement do a better job than the existing statement of defining the current and anticipated direction of the congregation?

5. Has the congregation identified values, areas of ministry, or goals that are not found in the proposed statement that the session/board should consider? What are they?

Thank everyone for coming. Offer praise for their work, and reassurance that the conversation will be taken into consideration when the board/session is making its final draft of the mission statement.

Session 6

Finalizing the Mission Statement and Vision Statement

For discussion:

1. What words, themes, and phrases came up at the congregational discussion that had not been previously discussed or explored?

2. Was the emphasis of the congregation similar, or dissimilar, to the conversations that were held by the board/session in meetings 1-4?

3. Did the congregation's assessment of areas of ministry reveal anything new? Were the outlined areas of ministry the same or different? Were the goals prioritized in the same way?

4. Are there any factors in the life of the congregation happening right now that would cause the congregation to focus on a particular topic or interest?

5. Overall, what was your sense of the congregation's response to your proposed mission statement?

6. What was your sense of the congregation's response to the previous mission statement?

Look at the draft of the mission and vison statement you created. Viewing it through the lens of the congregation conversation, should changes be made? Are there things that should be added, changed, or corrected?

Does it accurately summarize the hopes and desires of the whole body?

Is the mission statement a roadmap for the future?

Are the statements compelling?

Are you proud of the work you have done?

Has the workbook been helpful in building a mission and vision statement?

Conclusion

Congratulations on the completion of this workbook. Now, it's time to officially adopt the statements through the proper channels of your organization.

Once the statements are adopted, have a celebration with your congregation to officially adopt and begin to use the statements. Encourage each committee and area of ministry to use the statements as a guiding map for the life and future of your church.

Remember to share your adopted statements frequently so they become part of the life of the church!

As your church continues its ministry and mission in serving Jesus Christ, may you be richly blessed.

It is my hope that the workbook you have now completed has been helpful in the process of discerning your values for this time and place in your ministry. May the work you have completed will guide your church in ways that bless both its members and those outside your church walls.

About the Author

Rev. Jessica Crane Munoz is a Presbyterian Church (USA) minister serving at the Presbyterian Church of Vinton, Iowa. She has a B.A. from Concordia College, Moorhead, Minn. and a M.Div from Princeton Theological Seminary.

She has written one previous book "How I Roast Amazing Coffee At Home" that has nothing at all to do with church. It is available through Amazon.com.

Made in United States
Orlando, FL
16 April 2024